COGNITIVE BEHAVIORAL THERAPY

A Psychologist's Guide to Overcoming Depression, Anxiety & Intrusive Thought Patterns – Effective Techniques for Rewiring your Brain

Table of Contents

INTRODUCTION

Congratulations on getting a copy of *Cognitive Behavioral Therapy: A Psychologist's Guide to Overcoming Depression, Anxiety & Intrusive Thought Patterns – Effective Techniques for Rewiring your Brain*. If you are dealing with a mental health issue, then you know how difficult it can be to break free of the habits that it traps you in. Luckily, cognitive behavioral therapy, and its related forms of therapy, provides plenty of ways to do just that, regardless of what type of issues you may be dealing with in the moment. What's more, plenty of its techniques can be practiced without the help of a therapist and without diminishing the techniques' returns.

In order to help ensure that your treatment is as successful as possible, the following chapters will discuss the basics of CBT treatment as well as the mental health issues that are likely to see the most benefit from the practice. You will then learn all about cognitive distortions, one of the leading causes of the issues that CBT is adept at solving.

From there, you will get into the essence of the book, various alternatives to the more standard form of CBT, starting with a discussion of emotional triggers and dialectical behavior therapy. Next, you will learn how to deal with bad habits through multiple different approaches: acceptance and commitment therapy and functional analytic therapy. Then, you will learn about the ways you are connected to the world around you through multiple modality therapy before moving on to eye movement desensitization and reprocessing therapy. Finally, you will learn all about emotive behavior therapy.

There are plenty of books on this subject on the market. Thanks again for choosing this one! Every effort was made to ensure it is full of as much useful information as possible. Please enjoy!

CHAPTER 1

UNDERSTANDING CBT TREATMENT

Cognitive Behavioral Therapy (CBT) works based on the assumption that not all behaviors can be controlled by conscious thought and will alone. In fact, behaviors actually occur due to a mix of external and internal stimuli and years of conditioning in one way or another. While other types of therapy may be curious as to the deeper meanings behind your thoughts and actions, CBT is instead focused on getting results. It is all about understanding a specific issue you are dealing with and teaching you to manage it effectively using one or more of the exercises or adjacent therapy types discussed in these pages.

CBT was originally created as a way to help those who were dealing with depression specifically. It is a type of psychotherapy that has become extremely popular over the years, spawning numerous variations and gaining use for a wide variety of diverse mental issues. At its core, CBT's goal is to mitigate problems directly by locating negative behaviors, and their related thoughts, and changing them to something more beneficial. CBT is a mixture of behavior therapy and cognitive therapy and takes numerous principals from each.

When it comes to dealing with mental issues such as anxiety, depression and phobias, CBT views them as the result of some type of particularly harmful stimuli, combined with a variety of fearful avoidance responses that may or may not be automatic themselves. Issues that CBT is known to positively affect include psychotic disorders, nervous tics, eating disorders, dependence disorders, addiction, anxiety disorders, PTSD and mood swings. While this type of therapy is, naturally, not going to be the right choice for everyone, it has been proven to help those who are dealing with the outlined conditions more noticeably than psychodynamic therapy and other, more traditional options.

Modern CBT can trace its roots back to the types of behavioral therapy that were popular in the early part of the twentieth century. This type of therapy really became popular thanks to the widely popularized Pavlov's dogs experiment where a scientist proved that he could train dogs to salivate on command simply by ringing a bell and teaching the dogs to associate it with food. This idea was taken out of the realm of the parlor trick and first put to good use by another scientist by the name of Mary Jones who used a similar practice to successfully mitigate a variety of serious fears in children.

By the late 1950s, behavioral therapy was considered the most effective form of therapy for a wide variety of mental issues and was being practiced around the world. During this time, a therapist by the name of Aaron Berk was working on a theory that not all thoughts were formed consciously, which meant that thoughts could lead to emotions without the owner of both having any real say in the matter. This in turn led to the creation of what he named cognitive therapy as a means of learning more about automatic thoughts.

As behavioral therapy was not proving terribly effective when it came to dealing with depression, cognitive therapy caught on surprisingly quickly. As it continued to prove useful for a wider and wider variety of mental health issues, it became more popular as behavioral therapy started to fall out of favor.

As both types of therapy contained many similar behavioral aspects, while also focusing on the present and less on the underlying reasons behind specific thoughts and behaviors, many therapists began combining the two by the end of the decade. The two practices were forever joined in the 1980s when a pair of therapists named David Clark and David Barlow used a mix of both to develop a successful treatment for panic disorder.

Stages of CBT

The goal of CBT isn't to listen to each and every issue that you have going on in your life in an effort to diagnose you with a fancy sounding illness. Rather, it is to get to the root of the biggest problems in your life and find ways to make it easier for you to deal with them on a daily basis. The goal, then, can either be to change the way you think or to determine where specific maladaptive behaviors are located and work to squash them specifically.

The best way to go about doing so is through the use of a cognitive behavioral assessment which is made up of five key steps. First, you are going to want to determine the primary behaviors that are in play. Next, you are going to want to determine if the behaviors in question are either good or bad before then taking a look at the negative behaviors that you have uncovered in order to determine their frequency, duration and intensity. From there, you will want to determine the most beneficial course of action you can embark on in order to correct any relevant negative behaviors. Finally, you will want to determine how effective the treatment is and make changes accordingly.

Therapeutic alliance: This process is going to be overseen by a therapist, which means the first step to completing CBT successfully is to find a therapist whom you can form what is known as a therapeutic alliance with. This alliance is built on a relationship of mutual trust and respect, that can then be leveraged to generate solutions for the problems. This doesn't happen immediately, of course, and instead every CBT experience starts with a session where you and the therapist get to know one another. This is in an effort to decide if the relationship is going to be a good fit for everyone and to ensure that you get what you need from the process.

The therapist also uses this session to determine your current emotional, physical and mental state with the goal of getting to the root of your problems as quickly as possible. Your goal for the first session should be to feel positive about the person you have met and also about your overall chances for success with CBT. This is a crucial part of the overall experience, which means you aren't going to want to rush it. If you don't feel great about your new therapist by the time you leave their office for the first time, then you may want to give a few others a try, just to see what else is out there. This is a perfectly normal part of CBT, and you shouldn't be afraid to keep trying different therapists until you find the one that you know, beyond a shadow of a doubt, is right for you.

Learn to control your thoughts: Once you have established a therapeutic alliance, it will be time to start getting into what CBT is really all about. You and your therapist will discuss your problems, as well as how to go about solving them, starting with controlling your thought process. To do so, the first thing you will need to do is to come to an understanding in regard to how you think the way you do. As such, it is common at this time for you to discuss your past with your therapist, and how it connects to where you currently are in your life overall. Individual thought patterns that stem from an issue in the past and, in turn, affect the way you think and act currently are referred to as schemas, and isolating the negative ones floating around in your mind is crucial to your future success.

The other aspect of this stage you are going to want to keep in mind involves taking a closer look at your existing preconceptions and determining why it is that they may exist in your life in the first place. For this stage, it is also likely that your therapist will give you homework to complete. This will often include exercises to perform in hopes of changing negative thoughts into actions by creating new habits. This stage does not have a fixed time limit, and it will end when you have dealt with the issues that are causing you the most grief. Although, the average CBT treatment tends to last about 16 weeks with patients typically starting to see results after just a few weeks.

Create new patterns: After you begin to get control of your thoughts once more, your therapist will likely suggest ways you can develop positive thought patterns to replace the negative ones you have been removing from your life. This stage is all about practicing these new patterns until they become natural. You and your therapist will also brainstorm exercises that will allow you to strengthen and enhance the patterns that you are working on creating. If the previous step was about gaining control of your thoughts, this step is all about gaining control of your actions. It will be time to move on to the next stage when you find that you are able to use what you have learned appropriately, without consciously thinking about doing so.

Moving on: The final phase of your CBT journey will begin when you feel as though you are ready to manage your issues on your own, without the help of a therapist coaching you along every step of the way. This doesn't mean you are going to be done with your CBT treatment, however, it simply means that you will be taking control of your treatment and providing yourself the structure you need to remain successful at maintaining your new habits.

Unlike other forms of therapy, it is entirely possible to successfully practice CBT by yourself, as long as you take special care to ensure that you are promoting the right types of behavior first, to ensure you aren't accidentally doing more harm than good. This is why practicing with a therapist who specializes in CBT first is recommended as it ensures you learn good habits that you can simply stick with as opposed to creating new ones from scratch by yourself.

CBT can be successfully used in a wide variety of ways, including setting goals, creating new coping strategies, improving your relaxation techniques and various types of self-instruction. It can also effectively be used in a group setting or in one-on-one situations. CBT can also prove effective regardless of how long you practice it, though the longer you are able to do so, the more effective it will be in the long run.

Get the most from CBT

In order to ensure that you are able to get as much from CBT as possible, right from the start, there are multiple things you can do in order to ensure that you get started on the right foot.

Know what you are getting into: While there is never going to be a true substitute for meeting a potential therapist in person, that doesn't mean you can't improve your chances of finding someone you hit it off with right away. After taking a look at the types of CBT adjacent therapies discussed in this book, you should have a pretty good idea of the type of therapy that seems like it will be a good fit for you. Narrowing your list of potential therapists down to the specific subset of CBT that sounds right for you will save you a lot of time when compared to starting with a general CBT practitioner and working inwards from there.

It is also important that you take the time to read reviews of the therapists that you are considering, and also check to see what types of cases they deal with most regularly. If you are having trouble finding someone that seems like a good fit, ask around in your social circle, you may be surprised at just how many people have opinions on the matter.

Prepare yourself mentally: Even if you are open to the idea of CBT, change can be a difficult process to commit to fully. In order to ensure that you get the most out of CBT, it is important that you undertake the endeavor with determination and focus to ensure that you are able to follow through until the end. This means you are going to need to leave your comfort zone behind and never look back. In order to see the best results, you need to commit to not diving into the process halfway. You need to commit to the process of change fully in order to see the best results.

While there are plenty of different types of CBT discussed in the following chapters, it is important that you give each a fair shake before moving onto the next. Only spending a few days, or even a few weeks, on a new set of exercises is no way to truly test their efficacy. There is no reason to be in a rush when it comes to trying new types of treatment. They aren't going anywhere, and you never know what types of benefits you might see if you simply give them the time they need to fully materialize.

Finally, if you have been approaching whatever type of CBT you are experimenting with cautiously, you might find that jumping in with both feet is more likely to yield success. Studies show that giving yourself over to the process noticeably improves your ultimate chance of long term success. This isn't to say that you should prepare to be in therapy forever. In fact, setting a tentative end date for your current round of CBT can force you into making changes that otherwise might be put off indefinitely. Consider the context surrounding your plan for change, and determine if setting a timetable is right for you.

CHAPTER 2

COMMON ISSUES CBT DEALS WITH MOST EFFECTIVELY

Anxiety

While feeling anxious or nervous from time to time, during moments where you are unexpectedly called out to perform in front of your peer group, or when dealing with an unexpected financial worry, are perfectly fine. Some people feel this way constantly, and even minor issues can send the feelings of anxiety climbing ever higher. If you feel as though the anxiety you are experiencing goes above and beyond what can be considered normal, then you might be living with some type of undiagnosed anxiety disorder. Despite the serious toll that this can take on those who deal with it on a regular basis, it can be difficult to determine for yourself. This is largely because anxiety can take many different forms, and the line between normal and excessive can be difficult to determine precisely.

The most common example of an anxiety disorder is excessive worry over common occurrences. The trouble then becomes deciding on a level of worry that is "normal" and a level that is "excessive". When it comes to generalized anxiety disorder, the most common type of anxiety disorder, excessive does have a precise meaning. If you would say you have had anxious thoughts more than 50 percent of the time for the past six months, then you may be dealing with an undiagnosed anxiety disorder.

This anxiety needs to be severe enough that you would classify it as interfering with your daily life to the point that it is causing physical issues such as fatigue or stomach pain. If you don't feel as though your physical symptoms are all that severe, then you may still be dealing with generalized anxiety. It can also make itself known by causing extreme dysfunction in your everyday life.

Another crucial indicator that you may have an anxiety disorder is if you find yourself having a hard time sleeping at night. It may be that you are agitated or otherwise unable to stop thinking about certain things that need your attention, regardless if they are all that serious in the grand scheme of things. In fact, approximately 60 percent of all of the people who experience generalized anxiety experience these symptoms. Alternately, you might find that you fall asleep easily, but when you wake up, your mind is immediately filled with anxious thoughts that you have a hard time quieting.

One symptom of generalized anxiety that is easy to miss, especially if you have been living with it for a prolonged period of time, is excessive muscle tension. This can also be difficult to pin down as it will likely manifest for everyone in different ways. This could be anything from clenching your jaw, to hunching your shoulders to balling your fists. A related symptom that many people with generalized anxiety experience is a general dislike of being touched.

Panic attacks are another symptom that can be confusing for many people, simply because it is not one that everyone is going to experience. Instead, if you happen to experience panic attacks on a regular basis, and your triggers don't seem to be related to specific fears or sensations, then there is a fair chance that an anxiety disorder may be to blame.

Depression

While everyone feels a little depressed now and then, there is a serious difference between feeling down in the dumps from time to time and feeling a level of complete and utter despair that is so severe that it seems as though it is never going to end. Depression can make it virtually impossible to enjoy the good things in life, or even remember that the good things in life exist at all. When you are in the clenches of a depressive episode, even making it through to the end of the day can be a Herculean feat. The good news is that things can get better, and recognizing the symptoms and connecting them to yourself is a great first step.

Officially, depression is a common and debilitating mood disorder that is far more than simple sadness. Rather, depression changes the way that your mind processes common events and activities, altering the way it functions and you feel, in the process. If left untreated, it can interfere with your ability to work, eat, sleep and generally enjoy any facet of life. The feelings of hopelessness that it brings along can be so intense that it can seem impossible to believe that any relief is in sight.

If you do feel as though you are battling depression, the first thing you will want to do is to pay closer attention to your moods and emotions. If you are truly suffering from depression, then your brain will have a hard time regulating your emotions properly, which means you may find yourself dealing with extreme levels of guilt, hopelessness, despair, numbness and more. You may also feel as though you are worthless in general, though if you look for the source of these feelings, you will likely come up empty handed as well. You will also likely be more irritable than normal, which can result in a shortened temper and an increase in verbal or physical altercations.

Besides dealing with lots of unwanted emotions, you will also likely feel the need to withdraw from social activities that you previously enjoyed, along with your support group as well. Those who are battling undiagnosed depression often feel an urge to retreat from the world at large, in hopes that isolation will make what they are dealing with more manageable. This is rarely going to be a good choice, however. Without a means to connect to the outside world, the problems that they are dealing with tend to seem worse, not better, and then things are only magnified when they have no other viewpoint to listen to but their own.

If you still aren't sure if you are depressed, the next thing you are going to want to keep in mind is that you will likely be experiencing behavioral changes as well as mental ones. This does not mean that you are going to see these changes materialize all at once, however, and will instead slowly appear and grow more pronounced over time where you may not even notice them as a result. As such, you will likely find it helpful to track your behaviors over time to ensure any negative habits you are aware of don't get any worse, and no new ones appear at the same time.

Common signs of depression that you are going to want to be on the lookout for include erratic behavior such as either a dramatic increase or decrease in food consumption. Both over and undereating can be signs of depression, so if you notice a change in either direction, you may want to consider your overall mental state. You will also want to track your behaviors in order to make sure you aren't doing anything that could be considered a risky behavior. This could be obvious things such as taking up an interest in dangerous activities, or it could be something subtler, like an increase in consumption of drugs or alcohol. Either way, it represents an underlying desire to deal with the problems you are experiencing that is manifesting in the worst way possible. If you fail to reign in these types of issues soon, they can easily lead to long-lasting harm.

If, based on the above or your own personal experiences, you believe that you are dealing with depression, then it is extremely important that you remain ever vigilant when it comes to warding off suicidal thoughts. If you have even one thought that involves seriously considering self-harm or even suicide, then you should contact emergency services right away or call the Suicide Prevention Hotline as this can be a dangerous issue to attempt to deal with on your own. Regardless of how you feel in the moment, it is crucial that you keep in mind that things can get better and that there is help out there. All you need to do is look for it.

Phobias

Much like with anxiety and depression, feeling afraid from time to time is a perfectly natural experience. While fear in moderation is useful when it comes to keeping us alive and alert, a phobia extends that fear out in intense ways that are impossible to control. When experiencing a normal fear response, it is common to feel uncomfortable when you are around whatever it is that you are afraid of. For example, if you were afraid of air travel then the thought of being on an airplane might cause you to break out in a cold sweat, and being on an airplane might not be fun, but you could power through if flying was required.

If you had a phobia of flying, however, then it is unlikely you could even make it onto the airplane without a serious dose of tranquilizers, and even then, it still might not be something that you could manage on your own. Those with phobias will go to extreme lengths to avoid the thing that they are afraid of, which is why their fear can be so difficult to deal with on a regular basis. If you feel as though the thing you are afraid of could literally appear at any time, it can be difficult, if not impossible, to carry out many otherwise common tasks.

In addition to the severity of the fear in question, if you have reason to assume that you are suffering from a phobia, then you are going to want to consider where it came from in the first place. This will likely be where your CBT therapy should begin. If you are only afraid of something, then you likely won't need to worry about the source of the fear, except when you are being confronted by it directly. If you have a phobia, however, then you are likely afraid of the fear you feel as much as you are of the thing that triggers your phobia in the first place.

Those with a serious phobia often find themselves living in fear of anything and everything that is going to trigger an extreme panic response, often going so far as to alter every other part of their life in an effort to find a situation where they can exist in a more relaxed state. If they know they are going to have to come up against a potential trigger, it is likely all they can think about, and it is something that they dwell on well past the point of reason. They will also likely find that they have a hard time sleeping through the night, and when faced with their phobia, they find it consumes their thoughts completely.

CHAPTER 3

UNDERSTANDING COGNITIVE
DISTORTIONS

When it comes to the hierarchy of reliable information about the way the world works, those thoughts that come from within are, quite naturally, at the very top. After all, if you can't trust your own brain, then who can you trust? While you have learned to trust your own brain after years of using it to find solutions to everyday problems, alert you to danger, and even find a mate, not everything it is going to tell you is necessarily going to be about promoting your best interests.

In these instances, your brain won't be lying to you directly, it will just have gotten its wires crossed somewhere along the way. If these faulty or erroneous connections are not sorted out in relatively short order, they can solidify and start sending you faulty information which, in turn, can cause you to stop perceiving the way the world really is. Unfortunately, it is extremely easy to create these types of faulty connections, as the brain is naturally biased towards making connections between specific thoughts, consequences, actions and ideas, regardless of how connected these things might actually be.

Cognitive distortions explained

This propensity to make connections when there is no true link between two things often occurs as a result of misinterpreting research and assuming that correlation equals causation. This is all too easy to do, however, as it can be easy to see something that happens based on a coincidence, or only see part of a more complicated series of events, and make assumptions based on what you have seen. These assumptions are collectively known as cognitive distortions.

A cognitive distortion is a biased perspective that a person takes on about themselves or the world around them. At their heart, they are always irrational thoughts that are reinforced, either knowingly or unknowingly, over time. These patterns and systems of thoughts are often extremely subtle. So much so, that it can be difficult to recognize them because they are such a common part of your daily thoughts. This is exactly what makes them so potentially dangerous as it is exceedingly difficult to change things that you don't perceive as needing to be changed.

While cognitive distortions come in many different forms, they are all going to have some things in common, starting with the fact that they are all patterns or tendencies in belief or thought. They are also always going to contain the potential to cause psychological damage in addition to being patently inaccurate and false.

When first taking stock of your cognitive distortions, you may find it difficult or frightening that there is something out there that is influencing your thoughts without your conscious say in the matter. It is important to keep it up, however, as the only way you can ever hope to overcome your distortions is to shine the brightest light you possibly can on them. It is also important to keep in mind that dealing with multiple cognitive distortions at once is an exceedingly common incident. If you are human, you are going to experience them, it is as simple as that.

Broadly speaking, dealing with an extensive number of cognitive distortions all at the same time can indicate symptoms of depression. Erroneous thinking and cognitive distortions are particularly effective when it comes to exacerbating and proving the issues commonly associated with depression. It is still somewhat unknown if these distortions are brought on due to the depression, or if they form as a side effect of that depression. As such, while the exact relationship remains unclear, what is clear is that the two go hand in hand in some way, shape or form.

Common cognitive distortions

While there are countless different cognitive distortions and variations on cognitive distortions out there, the following list contains what are considered some of the most common.

Polarized thinking: Also known as all-or-nothing thinking, this type of cognitive distortion makes it difficult to see things in shades of gray, which makes all or nothing answers seem particularly attractive. This also manifests itself as seeing things at one end of the spectrum or the other; things are either amazing, or they are terrible, they are never just okay.

Overgeneralization: This type of cognitive distortion takes one example of a situation that has occurred and applies it to every instance of that situation, regardless of the specifics that were in play. Overgeneralization often leads to unwarranted negative thoughts, either external or internal, based on only a limited number of experiences.

Mental filter: The mental filter cognitive distortion tends to focus on a single negative aspect of a given situation and completely excludes all of the positives. A common example of this type of distortion occurs in a romantic relationship when one of the parties dwells on a negative comment made by the other, completely ignoring the years or decades of positive experiences they've shared. A mental filter cognitive distortion can make the entire world seem like a miserable place because one small facet is out of whack.

Disqualifying the positive: Similar to a mental filter, the disqualifying the positive cognitive distortion understands that positives have happened in relation to a specific situation, it just rejects them as false, regardless of the evidence that exists that shows they are the real deal. This is an especially dangerous cognitive distortion as it can sustain any number of negative thought patterns regardless of how much evidence mounts up to the contrary.

Jumping to conclusions (Mind reading): The jumping to conclusions cognitive distortion manifests as the inaccurate belief that we know what another person is thinking. Of course, it is possible to have an idea of what other people are thinking, but this distortion refers to the negative interpretations that we jump to. Seeing a stranger with an unpleasant expression and jumping to the conclusion that she is thinking something negative about you is an instance of this distortion.

Fortune Telling: The fortune telling cognitive distortion is similar to mind reading in that it refers to the common tendency to jump to conclusions and make predictions based on little or no evidence either for or against the assumption, and then defend these ill-founded beliefs to the death moving forward. A common example of this is anyone out there who is convinced that they are never going to find love simply because they haven't yet.

Minimization and magnification: The minimization and magnification cognitive distortion is also known as the binocular trick due to the way it can subtly influence your perceptions without you even realizing this is the case. It does this by either making unimportant things seem important or by greatly reducing the importance of otherwise meaningful things. It should come as no surprise that the things that are magnified are almost always negative, while the positive things are almost always minimized. For example, a student athlete who tends to function at the top of their game often magnifying the importance of every mistake they make while minimizing the accolades of their fellow players as meaningless.

Exercises to combat cognitive distortions

Decatastrophizing: This is a particularly useful exercise when your cognitive distortions have convinced you that the current situation, or an upcoming situation, is, or is going to be, a catastrophe. The first thing you are going to want to do is analyze the catastrophe using "what if" statements. You will also want to give the catastrophe a rating from 1 to 100.

Once you have put some limits on the catastrophe in question, the next thing you will want to do is to consider how likely it is that it is actually going to occur. A good place to start is going to be thinking back to similar incidents in the past and trying to remember if something akin to the catastrophe has happened previously. If it has happened before, you will want to determine just how often, so you can determine its likely frequency. With this done, you will be able to determine how likely the catastrophe is to occur right now. If it is under 30 percent, then it is considered statistically unlikely, and you have nothing to worry about.

If you have a reason to assume that the catastrophe is more likely to happen than not, the next thing you are going to need to do is consider how bad it is going to be. While the word catastrophe is being thrown around a lot in this chapter, it is entirely possible that the consequences you are dealing with are going to be minor, which also negates any urgency that worrying about it might require.

If the situation seems as though it is going to be bad, then you can work on coming up with a plan that will make dealing with the fallout as manageable as possible. You will want to think about the resources that you have at the ready and how you dealt with the issue before, if applicable. Making a list of everything at your disposal is a great way to not only see what you are working with, it is a great way to make you less anxious about the potential catastrophe as well.

The final step is going to be creating a narrative for yourself about how the catastrophe is going to go. Working through it step by step, you should be able to come up with a spin on it that makes the entire thing seem much more manageable. Once you have your story in mind, simply keep repeating it and get ready to face the future head on, secure that you have a plan if things go sideways.

Modifying assumptions: Another part of cognitive distortions are assumptions that we naturally feel as though we must live by. These rules or assumptions can make it easier to stick to a moral code, but they can also limit or frustrate us for no good reason. In order to get started with this exercise, the first thing you are going to want to do is to think about all of your assumptions in an effort to determine if they are valid and to determine which you are going to modify.

The second step is to determine how the assumption currently affects your daily life, in both positive and negative ways, if applicable. After you have determined the scope of its impact on you, you will then need to consider where it first came from. Don't worry if this is something you haven't thought about before; this is rarely the sort of thing that people question on their own. With this out of the way, you will then be able to compare its advantages and disadvantages, of which there may be more than one.

This is not to say that just because an assumption has an advantage it is a good one, however. On the contrary, it may mean that it is even more dangerous because it can more easily mask as something positive instead. As such, you are going to want to consider all of the pros and cons at play in a given decision in order to proceed confidently.

Finally, you are going to want to take another look at the things that you will have written down as a means for determining if the assumption in question is positive or negative. If you find out that your assumption is negative, you may want to consider coming up with an alternate that will serve you better in the short-term, regardless if this is a big modification or just a small change. However you decide to change the rule or assumption, the new version should maximize the advantages of the rule, minimize or limit the disadvantages, or both. Consider how you can put this new and improved rule into practice in your daily life.

CHAPTER 4

DEALING WITH EMOTIONAL TRIGGERS

Dialectical Behavior Therapy (DBT) is a variation of CBT that spends its time locating the emotional or mental triggers that tend to lead to harmful physical states including suicide and addiction. The core assumption of DBT is that everyone is always actively trying as hard as possible to do the right thing; they only fail because they don't have all the tools they need to succeed. These tools can take many forms, including the skills needed to function properly, the creation of positive influences or the removal of negative influences.

DBT was initially developed in the 1970s as a means of treating those who were dealing with habitual suicidal thoughts or were coping with a severe personality disorder. Since that time, DBT treatments have been expanded to also help those who are dealing with brain trauma, eating disorders and mood disorders. Currently, tests are underway to determine its efficacy when it comes to helping those who are dealing with extreme addiction issues and those who have been the victim of sexual abuse.

In DBT, the mind has three distinct states, the emotional mind, the reasonable mind and the wise mind, which exist in a Venn diagram-like state. The emotional mind is on one side, the reasonable mind is on the other, and the wise mind can be found in the space where the two overlap. The reasonable mind comes into play when decisions need to be made based on existing facts, the emotional mind is most useful when emotions are used to generate actions, and the wise mind is a balanced version of the two working together for the betterment of the whole. The goal of DBT techniques is to minimize the effects of the emotional and reasonable mind working alone and to maximize the amount of time that the wise mind is in control.

DBT makes use of a variety of common CBT techniques including emotional regulation, reality-testing, tolerance building, acceptance, mindfulness practices and cognitive techniques. Additionally, it focuses on imparting a number of relevant skills to those who are dealing with issues in the moment. These skills can be broken into two varieties: "how" skills and "what" skills. Together, they are used to provide the skills required to manage mental health issues on their own.

DBT Pillars

There are four primary pillars of DBT that are going to remain consistent between patients. They are:

Individual: A therapeutic alliance is the true key to success with any variation of CBT therapy. Additionally, you will be required to write down your day to day experiences in order to provide written confirmation that you are following your agreed upon treatment plan. Issues that you experience will then be rated on a scale of 1 to 10 to ensure that nothing you are experiencing is going to lead to physical harm. The therapist provides coaching with any of the skills that may be required in order to minimize negative episodes. Major issues are treated first, followed by those that are interfering with the rate at which treatment is moving forward. Finally, you will deal with the issues that are interfering with the less vital aspects of your life.

Group: Group study is an important part of the treatment plan because many of the coping skills you will be using will eventually need to be used around other people, and a place with plenty of like-minded individuals is a great place to start. Group meetings typically occur about once a week for as many as three hours. They give those who are practicing DBT the chance to interact with strangers while helping them improve their ability to be mindful, regulate their emotions and tolerate a wide variety of experiences outside of their control.

Team consultation: The team consultation allows the DBT therapist to get together with other professionals and discuss best practices while monitoring results.

On the go sessions: These are shorter than normal sessions that take place in a non-face-to-face situation, often while the client is experiencing some type of extreme trigger.

Skills

(What) Look around: The goal with this skill is to ensure that you are always taking note of the world at large, as well as the space within your own mind, as if you were a completely impartial observer. Only by taking an objective approach is it possible for rational courses of action to be decided upon. DBT recommends mindfulness meditation, along with more fully acknowledging both emotions and thoughts, while at the same time not interacting with the negative ones directly.

(What) Report: After looking around, both internally and externally, you are then going to want to write down the specifics without using any emotional statements to color the commentary. Keeping your descriptions as free from emotion as possible will make it far easier for you to look back on the past with an accurate eye, regardless of what is taking place in the present. Taking the time to write down a physical list can also make it easier to get in the habit of doing this on a regular basis. The additional required actions will give you something to hang your mental hat on when compared to simply typing words onto a screen.

(What) Remain active: The goal with this skill is to become more invested in the things that are going on around you, from moment to moment, as a means of keeping negative thoughts out. This doesn't mean that your mind must constantly be on the move, as long as what it is concerned with is productive and healthy. As such, you will find success with this skill if you make a conscious effort to give the task at hand your full attention to ensure that negative thoughts won't have room to sneak in.

(How) Refrain from judging: When reporting and looking, it is important to avoid also thinking about what is going on, especially when it comes to using binary constructs such as fair/unfair or good/bad. Rather, a more effective approach is to remain impartial

in order to gain a perspective on the world that is not tinged by feeling. You can assign labels to events after the fact, after you have all of the information you need to make the most effective solution in the moment, based on the rational observation you performed and the conclusions you drew as a result. If you make the mistake of labeling something too soon, you then run the risk of influencing how you are always going to think about the situation, making it practically impossible to be objective when looking back on the event in question.

(How) Slow down: Focusing on just one thing at a time naturally allows for a more focused moment to moment experience which, in turn, makes it far easier to prevent unhealthy emotions or thoughts from attacking your mind. Multitasking is an increasingly popular goal, despite the fact that many studies show that switching between tasks is actually an inferior way of completing tasks, when compared to just doing them one at a time. As such, to see dramatic results in this arena, put down the second screen, you will be surprised at how much it helps.

(How) Focus on the things that work: With all the potential for things to turn out in a less than ideal way, it can be easy to question the things that do happen the way they were supposed to as well. This is a slippery slope, however, and you will find that you are far better

off if you choose the path of least resistance as frequently as possible. While you likely have plenty of things that didn't work out quite the way you wanted them to in the past, once you have determined what exactly went wrong, these old scenarios don't have anything left to offer you. It is instead a better choice to focus on the things that went right. They will give you confidence about the future while also allowing you to study and learn from your past successes, so they are more easily repeatable in the future.

Distress tolerance

If you find yourself having a hard time working through a distressing situation without experiencing a high amount of anxiety, then there are several DBT techniques that you might find useful.

Radical acceptance: Radical acceptance is a healthy alternative to many habitual avoidance techniques that you can use when you come across a situation that, at face value, seems extremely unfair or otherwise completely out of your control. Rather than focusing on this injustice in the moment, you can instead practice accepting the negative situation as a fact and instead focusing your mental efforts on doing everything you can to solve the problem at hand.

It is important to keep in mind that there is a clear difference between accepting something and agreeing or approving of the way in which it is proceeding. Acceptance is the best solution when a situation seems completely beyond your control. For example, if you find out that you did not get the promotion that you were hoping for, an unhealthy, but extremely common, response is to blame your superiors for their shortsightedness. In reality, however, this solution does little to actively improve your situation, while also denying yourself an opportunity for growth.

If you instead utilized an approach based around radical acceptance, you would come to understand that there was someone who was more qualified for the position than you, and thus be motivated to work harder in the future to ensure that the next time a similar opportunity arises you will be a more natural choice. This option not only allows you to find a practical outlet for the feelings that you may have left over from the experience, it also prevents these negative feelings from multiplying.

Self-soothing: If you find yourself in a situation with a trigger that you simply cannot abide, and your only option seems to be having a panic or anxiety attack, then you may find it useful to distract yourself with alternative stimuli in order to short circuit the attack and help yourself self-correct. The specifics of what you do to take yourself out of the moment doesn't matter, as long as it serves to take your mind off of the negative emotion that is threatening to spill out.

You can start by doing something as simple as paying attention to what is around you, finding a calm spot to be by yourself temporarily, or even find something shiny to keep yourself entertained until the feeling passes. You may also find listening to music to be effective, getting a massage or even literally stopping to smell the roses. Finding something salty or sugary to eat will also give you a caloric boost that will often serve to get your mind on the right track.

ACCEPT: If using the information that your senses provide to you doesn't seem to be enough to snap you out of your heightened emotional state, the acronym ACCEPT can help you to get your mind off of the issue that is causing the negative reaction in the first place.

- Activities: Before your next attack hits, consider a variety of activities that you could have on hand that will require your full concentration to complete successfully. Focusing your concentration away from the inciting issue will help to make whatever your issue is that much more manageable.

- Contributing: Helping others is a great way to get your mind off of the issue that is causing the problems. While not always available, you may find that community service makes it easier to put your problems into perspective overall.

- Comparison: Regardless of how you feel about your current situation, it is likely that you have made it through worse in the past and have lived to tell the tale. As long as you can find a positive variation of the situation in question, then whatever you are facing at the moment should suddenly feel that much more manageable.

- Emotions: While not applicable in every situation, if you can find a way to force yourself to feel an emotion that is the opposite of whatever emotion the situation is causing you to feel, you can cancel out the panic or anxiety attack with ease.

- Pushing away: If you are familiar with mindfulness meditation, then you are familiar with the concept of perceiving thoughts without interacting with them, a great way to show your negative thoughts the door.

- Thoughts: If you feel your thoughts starting to take over, you may find it helpful to count backwards from 100 or to recite something you have memorized for just such an occasion. If you can ensure you keep control of your thoughts, then you can be sure they won't be taken over by emotions.

CHAPTER 5

DEALING WITH BAD HABITS

ACT

Acceptance and commitment therapy (ACT) was developed in the 1980s and is different from many of the other approaches to CBT. Rather than attempting to remove all negative feelings, it instead promotes positive growth. This is done by working with users to allow them to develop new behavioral patterns that are not based around dealing with the negative feeling in one way or another. This is achieved through a mixture of behavior altering strategies that are designed to increase commitment while also improving mental flexibility. ACT also promotes the process of becoming more aware of your negative thoughts and impulses through the act of learning to ignore them.

The end goal of ACT is to teach you how to control your sensations, memories, thoughts and feelings by becoming more aware of your negative thoughts while at the same time not interacting with them in any way. As such, ACT involves many different mindfulness mediation practices. These focus on remaining as fully in the present as possible while also making it easier for you to take positive action to get the things you want out of life.

Another thing that sets ACT apart is that it assumes that everyone has destructive thoughts. Those patients that other disciplines might label as maladjusted or mentally ill, simply have more of them or have a harder time controlling the ones they do have. It further believes that these issues are always caused by some mixture of an extremely rigid psyche, undue cognitive entanglement or an overdeveloped need for avoidance. This, in turn, prevents those who are dealing with it from cultivating the types of positive patterns that make it possible to behave productively.

Another thing that sets ACT apart from other types of CBT is the fact that it can be practiced just as effectively on your own as it can be with a licensed therapist. The goal is to be present in the moment, which is something that you can learn to do successfully by yourself. The physical repetition and minimal thought required when you are doing things like making breakfast, showering, exercising and more can all put you in the proper mindset to make being mindful easier than you might expect. Remember, being mindful is a skill, which means that it will only improve with practice.

The FEAR acronym outlines the way ACT defines the issue at the heart of most problems:

- Fuse together actions and thoughts

- Expand on one of your experiences

- Avoid the details that your senses are providing

- Reframe the situation so negative patterns make sense

- The opposite of FEAR, then, is ACT

- Accept the truth of what your senses are telling you in the moment

- Create a positive plan, and stick to it no matter what

- Time your plan to the moment when it will do the most good

ACT is made up of six steps, with the overall goal of teaching those who are in need to become more mentally flexible.

Diffuse cognitive distortions: The first step of ACT focuses on minimizing the natural tendency that many people have of returning to negative thoughts, emotions, memories or images, despite there being nothing to be gained by doing so. If you find yourself unable to resist returning to old thoughts time and again, then storing them in your mind palace might be an effective way to lock them up for good.

The mind palace technique works by allowing you to picture your mind as a large building with rooms dedicated to different types of thoughts. The floorplan of the building doesn't matter. What does matter is that it is a building that you can picture perfectly, down to the smallest detail. This aspect of the mind palace is crucial as the more realistic the building seems, the easier it will be for you to store your memories there. Once you have formed your mind palace, you are then going to want to place all of the memories you would rather not deal with behind a single door, and then wall that door over so that it can never be opened. While this might sound silly, you will be surprised at how effective it is in practice.

Be aware, don't interact: While a mind palace will help to remove negative thoughts that seem to stick around, there are always going to be those that appear as if from nowhere. Once you have accepted that this is something that is beyond your control, you will find it will be easier to divert these thoughts away from your mind, without directly interacting with them more than necessary. It is important to always remember that having thoughts of all types is perfectly normal; the thing that matters most is the way in which you react to them. If you force yourself to refrain from making negative judgements about yourself when these negative thoughts do appear, you will find that they are much easier to dismiss out of hand.

Be more in the moment: After you have started taking back control of your thoughts, you will find that this new mastery makes it easier for you to understand the smaller shifts in your existence. This means you are going to want to take into account everything your senses are trying to tell you, regardless of what is going on in the past or the future. The only thing that matters is the moment. You will likely find that it is easier to reach this mindset in a quiet place at first, though eventually, you will be able to reach it virtually anywhere.

The easiest way of going about ensuring that this is the case is by listening to what your body is trying to tell you. Your mind filters out a constant barrage of information from your senses on a near constant basis. This filter can be removed, however, if you make a conscious decision to do so, and all of that information can be accessed directly. For example, if you simply take the time to focus on the way that the clothes you are currently wearing feel against your skin, then you will find that there is a wealth of sensory data just waiting to be unpacked.

Face inward: You will find that if you can stop putting so much focus on either the future or the past, then it becomes much easier to look at yourself with a critical eye, and therefore, find the easiest path to your goals. This will make it easier for you to determine the difference between reality as you currently see it and the way it actually is. If you take the time to really study these differences, then you will find that you are able to more easily see when your mind is creating unnecessary static, and when there are actually things in your way that are preventing your success.

Study the patterns: After you have been made aware of your goals and decided on the best way to achieve them, you will likely notice that it is becoming easier for you to pick out general patterns in your behavior as well. In turn, viewing these patterns as a whole will make it easier for you to determine the true values that are closest to your heart. Understanding what values these are, beyond a shadow of a doubt, will make it easier for you to determine what your common patterns are as well.

While it is important to consider your common patterns, it is equally important to not go overboard on the process. Remember, the human brain likes patterns, so much so, that it will often go out of its way to find them even where they don't exist. When poking and pointing at your psyche, don't go overboard. Sometimes you won't be able to find patterns, and that is perfectly fine as well.

Put it to use: After you have a clear idea of what your goals and values are, it should make the path ahead of you much easier to figure out. All that will remain at that point, is to move forward with the things you have learned, continue to promote positive habits and use them effectively. While this will likely seem easier said than done at first, each time you act on the things you have learned it will make the next action a little easier to make. Slowly, but surely, this will cause new habits to form.

FAT

Functional analytic therapy (FAT) is another variation on the more common type of CBT that places the majority of its focus on the therapeutic alliance itself as it believes this to be the most effective catalyst to change in the patient's life at the moment. Specifically, the FAT therapist will work with the patient through the use of what is known as contingent responding, wherein they bring up specific, positive behaviors and responses that encourage positive behaviors to continue. At the same time, they will be downplaying the use of negative or coping behaviors. This process involves a lot of active listening on the part of the therapist, which is useful when it comes to reinforcing positive behaviors even more. This approach allows the patient to feel as if they are in control at all times, which naturally leads to more personal breakthroughs as well.

The idea at the core of FAT therapy is that the sooner that an outside party, in this case, the therapist, is able to point out negative behaviors and offer up real alternatives, the easier it will be for the patient to use a more positive alternative instead. The reason that changing habits remains so difficult is that any regret you might feel about a habit, and thus any desire to change, takes place well after the inciting incident occurs.

The subconscious mind can be thought of as an untrained puppy in that it requires direct, immediate feedback in order to ensure that positive change not only happens once, but keeps happening moving forward as well. Luckily, the suggestions that are made by a therapist are naturally going to be more effective than those you have yourself, as the therapist is in a situation of authority in this situation. This will cause your mind to spend less time questioning whether or not what they say is correct.

This is why FAT focuses so thoroughly on the relationship that is formed between the patient and the therapist. If this relationship is nurtured in the right way, then it is possible that clients will experience the thoughts and emotions associated with their problem behaviors as clearly as they would when they are experienced out in the real world. Patients are also taught a variety of useful behaviors that they can focus on which are results based, regardless of how well the action is performed, to ensure that additional positive reinforcement is always right around the corner.

CHAPTER 6

UNDERSTANDING THE WAYS YOU CONNECT WITH THE WORLD

If you are interested in learning more about the ways in which you connect with the world around you, then the CBT adjacent therapy known as multimodal therapy is for you. This type of therapy focuses on the way that individuals think, feel, act, imagine and interact with the world around them with the goal of treating the issues associated with CBT through a variety of modalities that are tailored towards each specific issue. It also posits that each person contains all of the modalities that are discussed below within them. The only difference is the way each affects them personally based on a variety of different internal and external factors.

Multimodal therapy is a variation on the classical conditioning model and is known to be effective when it comes to treating a wide variety of mental disorders including chronic pain, insomnia, low self-esteem, compulsions, stress management, emotional eating, weight problems, chronic relationship issues, social anxiety disorder, panic issues, depression, anxiety, PTSD and more.

Modalities to be aware of

Behavior: The behavior modality is expressed most commonly via negative habits and gestures, along with acts that are known to be inappropriate. It is important to keep in mind that positive behaviors can be just as revealing as the negative ones, however, and the full range of behaviors includes destructive, constructive, immoral, moral, mature, childish, appropriate, inappropriate, legal, illegal, impulsive and restrained. While the natural response is likely going to be to deal with the behavior directly, this is not going to affect the root issue, and so the behavior is likely to continue.

Affect: The affect modality can be thought of as the degree of intensity that you ultimately associate with the emotions and feelings that you experience and the amount of control you feel you have over them as a result. This is one of the most commonly misaligned modalities, and the one that most people are more naturally aware of. These feelings are often tied directly into the greater modal framework, which means fixing them is often more complex than simply discussing them in-depth.

Sensation: The sensation modality refers to the physical characteristics that manifest in relation to a specific, external stimulus. This often includes things such as tension, pain, nausea, sweating and an increased heartrate. While these are the most common physical sensations, not all sensations are going to be physical, they could instead be hallucinations, illusions or sensations that you anticipate dealing with in the future. Sensation is often connected to the other modalities due to the fact that undesired sensations are often modified by mental means such as denial, or by physical means including drugs and alcohol.

Imagery: The imagery modality typically refers to the mental images that become associated with certain stimuli over time. This often includes things like daydreams, fantasies and nightmares, along with your self-image and therefore, your self-esteem as well. Anxiety and depression are the issues most commonly associated with this modality, and those who experience either one of these especially vividly often find themselves conjuring up worst-case scenarios without even meaning to do so. As such, learning to modify the things you picture, instead of letting them lead you along blindly, is going to be an important start of moderating this modality once and for all.

Cognition: The cognition modality covers additional attitudes, thoughts and beliefs that may cause you to feel a specific way about a certain issue. Deeply held values and self-talk fall under the purview of this modality as cognition is the modality that is most responsible for tying all of the other modalities together. If you are dealing with issues associated with body image disorder, depression or anxiety, then you likely need to adjust your cognition modality.

Interpersonal relationships: The interpersonal relationship modality relates to the way that a person forms support structures based on their social skills. It also affects your ability to feel connected to the people in your life, and thus, is key to fostering healthy and productive relationships. This, in turn, can be considered a crucial aspect of mental health in general. Feelings of isolation can often lead to the existence of other issues that may cause those who are dealing with them to feel the need to seek help at some point. Relationship issues are also known to link issues of otherwise unassociated modalities together.

Dependence: The dependence modality refers to any emotional or chemical dependencies that you might have, regardless of the reasons for their existence. It is also often related to the reasoning behind your specific drug of choice (if any). Also included in this modality are habits that tend to lead to the behavior in question; they typically fall into the dietary or habits categories.

While everyone is going to be affected by their modalities to some degree, the end results can typically be broken down into one of three categories based on how those dealing with them tend to approach problem solving. In general, people are either going to approach their problems with the intent of dealing with them on their own; they call their support network for help or they call on an outside source to substitute in for their support group. Once the source of the response is located, effective treatment can begin.

MMT session breakdown

Modality treatment is typically based on what is known as a life history inventory. This inventory covers a variety of relevant information and is filled out by the client during the first session.

- *General personal information:* As the name implies, this is all basic information including past treatment history.

- *History:* Family history including siblings, relationship with parents, parents' attitudes and habits, home life, education and reoccurring childhood issues.

- *Current problems:* This is a list of issues that are currently presenting problems in the client's life. This section also includes what the client hopes to get out of therapy, a list of the different modalities and a way to assess the current status of each.

With this assessment out of the way, the early stages of MMT therapy are going to proceed in a similar fashion to any other type of CBT, starting with a focus on creating the type of successful therapeutic alliance that can form a reliable foundation upon which future treatment can be based. The biggest difference between MMT and more traditional CBT is that it makes use of a number of questionnaires as a means of assessing which modalities are currently affecting you, how this affects you day-to-day and why this is the case in the first place.

Depending on the issues that you are currently dealing with, you may receive a recommendation from your therapist in terms of dietary suggestions, stress reduction options and relaxation tapes. The goal during the early stages will be to start generating a measurable benefit as quickly as possible, to make it easier to commit to the more difficult changes that will need to be made in the future. MMT sessions are often taped, with the consent of the patient, of course, as listening to sessions after the fact is often useful when it comes to getting new habits to stick.

From there, the MMT therapist works to ensure that each modality is functioning properly, offering suggestions for ways that existing issues can be mitigated. What follows is an example of how MMT might be used to help someone who is dealing with depression.

Behavior: If the client is having trouble getting out of bed on a regular basis, and as such, has grown disconnected from many facets of their life, then MMT would suggest setting daily goals as a means of connecting with the world once more. This would then progress to reestablishing social ties and a precise scheduling of the entire day until the habit of functioning as normal returns.

Affect: Assuming that the client's issues with depression were based on incorrectly based feelings of guilt at the death of a parent (through no fault of the client), then the MMT therapist would likely probe the triggers that are associated with the guilt. Once the triggers are revealed, the MMT therapist would then likely recommend some sort of exposure therapy to help the client confront their feelings of grief and put them in the past where they belong.

Sensation: If the depression is having the opposite affect on the client and is actually causing them to have difficult sleeping, then the MMT therapist will likely recommend a variety of relaxation exercises including proper breathing techniques and mindfulness meditation, possibly even self-hypnosis, to help ensure that they get a good night's sleep.

Imagery: If the client is experiencing issues with their self-image that is leading to their depression, or if they are having trouble viewing the future in a positive way, then the MMT therapist would work to help them to replace the negative thoughts they are experiencing with positive alternatives instead. This would be done through a variety of CBT-based techniques.

Cognition: If the client is using their depression as a filter through which to view the rest of the world, then this is a classic example of a cognitive distortion and the therapist would then offer up alternative methods by which to view the situation without having the bias stuck to it.

Interpersonal relationships: As the client in this example is missing out on interpersonal contact as a result of their depression, the MMT therapist would focus on ways to remind the patient of the importance of their support group as well as offer up assertiveness exercises and other ways to initiate positive social interactions.

Dependence: If the client is known to use prescription or nonprescription drugs to make themselves feel better, then MMT will make it a point to monitor and moderate use until a more permanent solution can be found.

Treat Yourself

In order to get started with MMT yourself, the first thing you are going to want to do is to consider the modalities listed above and determine which in your own life appear to be out of whack. From there, you will want to determine where you want to start, keeping in mind that starting with something that you can easily change will give you the confidence to work on something more serious.

In order to track your modalities, the most effective way to go about doing so is by keeping a journal of the experiences you have throughout the day and faithfully chronicling them each evening. When you are taking note of your daily activities, in addition to all the relevant details, you are also going to want to include how the situation made you feel, what you did in response and what the results were. Finally, you will want to include alternatives that would have likely led to a more positive result.

At first, you may have difficulty remembering everything that you do throughout the day, which is why you may want to write things down as soon as they have happened before transferring them to your journal at the end of the day. It is important to keep your notes in a physical notebook, not in a text document, as giving your feelings a physical presence can make them easier to deal with.

While at first you may not find your journal to be useful, once you stick with it regularly for at least a few weeks, you will find that it allows you to more readily see the common patterns that you live your life by, as well as if these patterns are positive or negative overall. With this done, determining which modalities you need to work on is as simple as looking at the negative patterns you find yourself in time and again and considering what modality should most likely be the cause. Be honest with yourself, and you will get to the bottom of your problems in no-time flat.

CHAPTER 7

DESENSITIZATION THERAPY

Eye Movement Desensitization and Reprocessing Therapy is a variation of CBT that has proven especially effective for those who are dealing with a wide variety of different mental health issues. It allows them to form more effective types of coping mechanisms than whatever they are currently using to deal with their underlying issues.

First created in the 1980s, EMDRT is based on the fact that everyone uses the same basic eye patterns when it comes to remembering trauma, either real or imagined, which means that by changing the movements of the eyes during this period, the intensity of the experience in question can change as well.

EMDRT is the most successful when it comes to dealing with PTSD, somatic disorders and personality disorders. It is different than a majority of the CBT exercises out there as it can be just as effective for children as it can be for adults. While it took some time to catch on in a real way, for the past decade, EMDRT has being rapidly gaining popularity.

One major reason for this increase in popularity is due to the fact that patients are able to often start seeing a noticeable improvement after just three, 90-minute sessions. This efficacy is improved to 100 percent among single-trauma cases and 70 percent in multi-trauma scenarios when treatment is instead spread out over six sessions.

How it works

EMDRT works through an extremely structured eight step process that looks at both the past, present and future ramifications of the negative or otherwise stressful memories that you might have. These steps are outlined here for discussion purposes, but it is important that the process is only practiced by those who are specifically trained in EMDRT, as otherwise it is possible to accidentally do far more harm than good.

(Treatment and History) Planning: This is a fairly straightforward step and includes a detailed history as well as an evaluation of the issue

in question. However, unlike most types of CBT, EMDRT is extremely interested in the things the client has experienced in the past. These distressing memories are then tagged as potential targets for reprocessing during a later step. EMDRT typically focuses on the most damaging experiences first, before moving on to milder memories. Starting with the most serious memories first will ensure that the client is able to see a serious change right from the start.

Proper relaxation techniques: Another important EMDRT tenant is remaining as calm as possible between sessions to ensure you keep your eye movements to a minimum before you learn to control them completely. Mindfulness meditation and guided imagery are both frequently used to get the client into an appropriate mindset. While many forms of CBT can directly benefit from mindfulness meditation when practiced in the home, EMDRT can benefit from its usage virtually anywhere. The ability to slip into a mindful state almost at will can make controlling your eye movements far more manageable.

VOC Scale: The VOC Scale, otherwise known as the Validity of Cognition Scale, is what is used to calibrate a person who is going to be using EMDRT for the first time. Initially, the patient will be asked to think of a specific image that they can relate negatively to, before then doing the same thing with a positive image instead. The patient will then be asked to consider how completely they believe in the positive image, followed by the negative image. They will then be asked to list any feelings that the images might generate as well as their overall level of intensity. They will finally be asked to link those sensations with various parts of the body, if relevant.

Reprocessing: The reprocessing step of EMDRT focuses on retraining the brain in order to experience positive emotions as opposed to the negative ones that are currently associated with specific memories. As a part of this exercise, the client will focus on trouble spots for about a minute at a time. While doing so, they will also be asked to focus on something that will cause them to look either left or right, as opposed to in the way that is currently associated with the negative memory in question.

The nature of the added stimulus isn't important. What is important is that it remains in play long enough for the eye movement to be moved away from the trouble spot. During each sessions the patient's eyes will be moved further and further from the trouble spot, improving their reaction to it in the process.

Improve beliefs: Once reprocessing has occurred a few times, the next step will be for the patient to retain the new patterns by relating back to the positive thoughts they generated earlier. This part of the process will also include another round of the stimulus from the previous step to ensure that future negative memories generate the same mitigated response. During this step it is crucial that the patient focuses on each part of the new emotion, including how it makes them feel both mentally and physically. After they have a strong grasp on the emotion, they will then be instructed to think about it in conjunction with the stimuli in question with enough conviction that the two become interconnected in their mind.

Track down remaining negative sensations: Once the most serious issues are dealt with, the therapist will then move on to any additional trouble spots that might remain outside of their scope. This often manifests itself as a type of tension, or tightness, or possibly another type of sensation that feels as though it is out of place. This is a result of the body redistributing signals as a result of the EMDRT and can be reduced with the additional application of relevant stimuli. This process is then repeated as needed to clean up any lingering physical or mental sensations.

It is important to not be so anxious to move through the steps of EMDRT that you blow through this step too quickly, as the physical effects of altered emotional responses can take some time to manifest themselves once the initial issues themselves have been dealt with. Additionally, during this period, you are going to want to perform the following mild exercises daily, to determine if any potential sore spots or uncalled-for stiffness persists longer than it should. This can easily be a sign of something larger than only EMDRT can fix.

- Step touches: You are going to want to perform this exercise for one minute, completing as many repetitions as possible. To begin, simply stand with your hands on your hips and then step to the side with your dominant foot before bringing your other foot out to meet it. You will then want to move in the opposite direction so that you end up back where you started. You can hold your hands above your head for extra intensity.

- Windmills: You are going to want to perform this exercise for one minute, completing as many repetitions as possible. Stand with your feet spread wide before bending at the waist and using your right hand to touch the floor near your left foot. Return to the starting position before doing the same with the left hand and the right foot. Repeat this process as many times as possible in a minute, going as quickly as possible without putting undo strain on the back. If you can't touch the floor to start, don't worry, simply get as low as possible and work on extending your reach in time.

- Knee smashers: You are going to want to perform this exercise for one minute, completing as many repetitions as possible. Start in a relaxed standing position with your arms bent at the elbow and held straight out in front of you. You will then want to raise your left knee and bring it up towards the right side of your chest, while at the same time bringing your forearm down upon it. Return to the starting position, and then repeat with the other arm and leg.

- Lunge and front kick: You are going to want to perform this exercise for one minute. Start in a relaxed standing position before dropping into a straight lunge position that is deep enough so that you can touch the floor. As you stand, you are going to want to bring your back leg up into a snap kick before returning to the starting position. Repeat with the other arm and leg.

- Squat pushups: You are going to want to perform this exercise for one minute. Start in a squatting position before walking yourself out into a pushup position using your hands for balance. Once in position, complete a standard pushup before walking yourself back into a squatting position. Finish with a jump before returning to the starting position.

Keep a log: Once the majority of a given issue has been dealt with, the patient is encouraged to keep a log of their experiences between EMDRT sessions to make it easier to determine when a trouble spot occurs in their daily life. This is due to the fact that it is critical for EMDRT to be used on every facet of the thought or action. The only way for EMDRT to be truly effective is by completely retraining the mind to act differently at an automatic level when presented with previous triggers. Most people find greater success when using a physical log as opposed to a digital one as it makes their issues feel more real, and thus easier to overcome.

Reassess: In response to the provided log, the therapist will then be able to determine if and when a specific trouble spot has been dealt with completely. Part of ensuring that these trouble spots are not going to return is to ensure that the patient is maintaining a positive routine, well past the point that the original negative behavior has long-since disappeared.

Practice for yourself

DIY EMDRT: While practicing the official EMDRT process described above without the proper training can lead to issues, there are some variations of the practice that you can use on yourself to see if you feel you would benefit from a more involved and formal process. To get started, all you need to do is to start with your relaxation technique of choice before thinking about the major emotional events that have taken place in your life. When you think of these memories you are going to want to do everything you can to place yourself within them, the more detailed the imagery, the better.

Once you have the negative image in your mind, switch to one that is extremely positive, shifting your eyes as you do so. Then, while thinking about the positive memory, you are going to want to move your eyes back and forth as though you were reading a book. You will then want to rotate between the two memories for as long as you can maintain your full concentration.

After a few weeks, you will likely feel as though you are starting to feel somewhat more positive about your negative memories. When this occurs, you are going to want to latch on to these new feelings and focus on growing them as much as possible to get them to stick.

71

The longer you focus on replacing your old feelings with the new, the better.

Butterfly hug: This is a useful self-treatment that can be used when feelings of anxiety or panic set in. Initially, you are going to want to focus on these feelings to the exclusion of everything else, while at the same time placing both of your hands onto your forearms, almost as if you were about to give yourself a hug. Instead, you are going to want to close your eyes and then tap on your forearms lightly, alternating between one and another.

Keeping your eyes closed, you are then going to want to visualize yourself completely removed from the stressful situation that you currently find yourself in, tapping away all the while. You will then want to keep it up until the negative feelings have dissipated completely, and then make a mental note of how effective the process was. With enough positive reinforcement, the tapping should be enough to completely mitigate any oncoming anxiety or panic attacks, while at the same time using the exercise to pinpoint the triggering event with extreme accuracy.

CHAPTER 8

RATIONAL EMOTIVE BEHAVIOR THERAPY

Rational emotive behavior therapy (REBT) treats patients based on the theory that people do not become emotionally disturbed just by being exposed to precise negative circumstances. Rather, they tend to develop emotional issues based on how they view these experiences when they look at them later in life through the lens of experience, language, beliefs and personal philosophy that reflects the way they see the world at large.

A to C psychological disturbance model

The A to C psychological disturbance model states that A (the incident that incites the trauma) does not directly cause C (the dysfunction) but results from B (people) taking the wrong meanings from A and acting based on those assumptions. In this equation, A can be virtually anything including events that haven't happened yet and only seem like a possibility thanks to the issues you are dealing with at the time.

As such, the beliefs that people have, as well as the reasoning behind them, are of the upmost importance for this type of CBT adjacent therapy. The more interrelated a belief is when it comes to influencing other beliefs, the more important it becomes overall, and the more you are likely to benefit by taking a closer look at it. When beliefs about actions are fictional and dysfunctional, absolute and rigid, then they are most likely going to be self-defeating and destructive as well. However, at the same time, incorrect beliefs can be beneficial if they are preferential, flexible and constructive as they can then still lead to patterns of behavior that are positive overall.

REBT theorizes that everyone has a mix of irrational negative tendencies and rational positive tendencies that they use to get through the day. Additionally, it posits that the irrational tendencies typically lead to the types of mental constructs that often promote addiction, avoidance, compulsiveness, procrastination, anxiety, depression, shame, guilt, hurt, anger, self-pity or self-blame.

In situations like these, REBT can often prove to be an especially useful educational tool that can help users to become adept at spotting defeatist and irrational thoughts and questioning them directly as a means of deactivating them and replacing them with positive alternatives instead. This, in turn, makes it easier for these thoughts to be cut off at the source and replaced with positive alternatives.

Thus, the ultimate goal of REBT can be seen as bringing about a personal realization that when unfortunate events occur in the future, it is possible to look at them in either a negative way, that can then easily lead to additional unproductive actions, or in a positive way that promotes productive change in the future. Over time, these positive ideas will then become more and more ingrained, and thus, a more effective barrier against the previous negative impulse.

Common negative beliefs

REBT tends to focus on three main negative beliefs that you are going to want to avoid at all costs in order to improve your overall positive outlook. The first of these is the idea that success is the only option, as anything else will lead to a loss of social standing, love and affection from your support group and the other good things in your life. As such, failure is seen as the worst possible outcome.

If you hold onto this idea, then when you find yourself dealing with adversity, you will often find yourself more depressed and prone to a greater frequency of anxiety or panic attacks than you may otherwise experience. This, in turn, often leads to an overall feeling of worthlessness that makes it difficult, or even impossible, to complete otherwise minor tasks.

The second belief that REBT focuses on shutting down relates to the way you feel about your personal space, specifically how it needs to remain under your control at all times. If you find that if something is out of place, then everything around you feels off, and you cannot rest until order is restored, then you might be dealing with this belief. When they find themselves faced with adversity, those who hold onto this belief will often find that they are suffering from fits of inaction, procrastination, avoidance, frustration, discomfort, intolerance, self-pity and anger. Additionally, those who are dealing with this belief find it much more difficult to stop and smell the roses as they are constantly being pushed by their beliefs to do something to improve the balance of the universe.

Finally, the third and final belief that REBT tries to snuff out relates to the way that others interact with you. If you feel as though the people around you must be nice to you at all times or you start questioning whether they ever liked you at all, then you may be dealing with this negative belief. If you are dealing with this issue, then you may find that when faced with adversity you regularly experience periods of anger, rage, fury and vindictiveness. What's worse, holding onto this idea for a prolonged period of time often makes it more difficult to form the types of support groups that promote a well-adjusted mental state.

Practice REBT

Fear of failure: While every variation of traditional CBT is going to be more effective with the help of a licensed therapist, there are still things you can do for yourself that have the potential to generate real results. If you are dealing with the belief that success is the only option when it comes to preventing bad things from happening in your life, then it is important to understand what issues you are transferring onto the idea of success.

The best way of doing so is going to be through tracing your fear back to its source. If you can trace your general sense that failure is the absolute worst possible outcome back to the incident that caused you to feel that way in the first place, then it may be easier to realize that failure is something that happens to everyone, and that it rarely leads to anything all that life altering.

Then, once you manage to reach the true heart of the matter, you will be able to focus on the heart of the problem with a critical eye, making it easier to solve any related problems that you may have been avoiding. You may also want to start keeping a journal of activities that you try, and fail to succeed at, so that you can refer to it at a later date to remind yourself that failure is not the end of the world.

Desire for control: If you find yourself spiraling out of control because you are unable to control every aspect of your personal space, then you may find that decatastrophizing is an effective way to put your desires into a broader context to see that they aren't actually based on any anything concrete, or are even all that relevant. As you grow better at noticing these types of cognitive distortions, you will find that they are rarely an accurate representation of the world as it really is.

To put decatastrophizing to work for you, all you are going to need to do is to stop and consider what might happen if your needs and desires are not met in a reasonable period of time. Rather than shying away from the anxiety that not having everything under your control causes, you are going to want to go deep with it, as deep as possible. You are going to want to look into every shadowy corner of your mind and poke at all the absolute worst-case scenarios that you can find, the more the merrier. When looking at these possible outcomes, what you are likely to find in most scenarios is that the worst thing that could really happen really isn't that bad. As such, as long as what you come up with doesn't involve death or dismemberment, then you are likely good to go.

As a rule of thumb, when you are making use of this technique, you will typically find that everything you are afraid of coming to pass isn't really anything that is serious enough to worry about. This, in turn, will not only make it easier to put aside many of the fears you have been harboring, it will also make it far easier for you to put them aside in the long-term, to never bother you again. Regardless, with practice, you should be able to perform this exercise in the moment, which means it will do wonders for helping you move forward with a clear head.

Irrational thoughts: If you find yourself automatically jumping to the worst conclusions possible about those you interact with on a daily basis, then a process known as Socratic questioning can be useful when it comes to getting you back on the right track. Based on the teachings of the ancient philosopher, Socrates, the goal of this exercise is to use a basic group of questions to explore the complicated beliefs that underline these types of assumptions. Using this method should help you to determine if you are responding to a situation accurately, or if you are viewing the situation through the filter created by a cognitive bias. Once you are aware of your inaccurate thoughts, it will then be much easier to pay them no mind.

To ensure this is not the case, ask yourself the following questions:

- Am I reacting the way I am for a specific reason, or is it just a force of habit?

- Am I looking at a complex situation in a way that is overly simplified?

- What evidence supports this thought?

- Am I basing this thought on facts, or is it simply based on feelings?

- Is this thought realistic based on any available evidence?

When working your way through these questions, it is important to take your time and really think about your answers, not simply rush through to say you gave them. Keep in mind that, when explored fully, these questions can really help you, but only if you take the time to consider the situation accurately in the first place. This means you may need to spend a few minutes on each question in order to ensure that you come up with the best answers possible.

With practice, the amount of time required will likely decrease, and you will also feel the need to use the process less frequently as your answers are often going to come out the same.

CONCLUSION

Thank you for making it through to the end of *Cognitive Behavioral Therapy: A Psychologist's Guide to Overcoming Depression, Anxiety & Intrusive Thought Patterns – Effective Techniques for Rewiring your Brain.* Let's hope it was informative and able to provide you with all of the tools you need to achieve your goals. Just because you've finished this book doesn't mean there is nothing left to learn on the topic; expanding your horizons is the only way to find the mastery you seek. Likewise, if you hope to make the most out of your time with CBT, you are going to need to become a lifelong learner on the topic. If you allow yourself to become satisfied with your achievements, then you risk backsliding and putting all your hard work at risk.

Above all, however, it is important to keep in mind that there are still plenty of different CBT exercises and techniques out there that were not covered in the preceding chapters. If you haven't found the right one for you yet, keep at it; you never know when the next exercise is going to be the one that's right for you. With that being said, however, it is important to not rush through the exercises listed here, but to give them each the amount of time required to ensure that they actually work for you or not, before moving on to the next.

While it can be easy to be anxious to try as many different types of CBT exercises as possible, it is important to keep in mind that finding the right solution to your problem is a marathon, not a sprint, which means that slow and steady wins the race. The more time that you give yourself to find the type of CBT that works for you, the more well-adjusted you will end up being in the long run.

Finally, if you found this book useful in any way, a review is always appreciated!

Made in the USA
Middletown, DE
18 February 2018